10 DAYS IN SCOTLAND

From Castles to Coastlines, A
Decade's Worth of Scottish Splendor
in 10 Days

TRAVEL TALES

Table of Contents

CHAPTER 10 Day 10

FAREWELL TO SCOTLAND

SCOTLAND

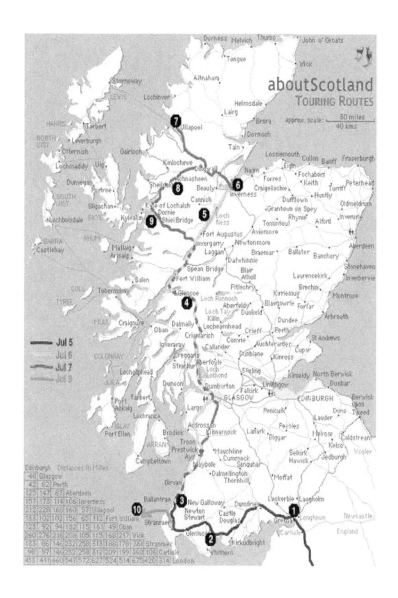

Scottish Highlands

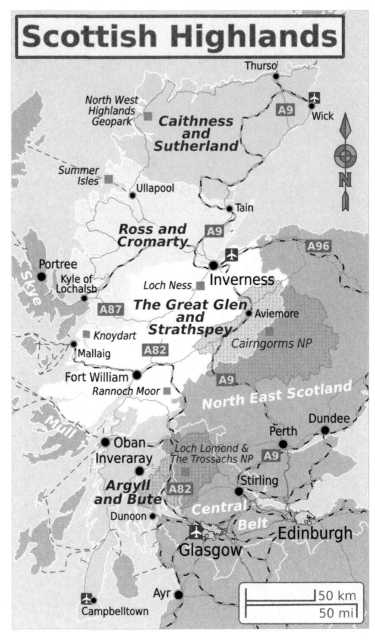

Thurso
North West Highlands Geopark
Caithness and Sutherland
A9
Wick
Summer Isles
Ullapool
Tain
Ross and Cromarty
A9
A96
Portree
Skye
Kyle of Lochalsh
Loch Ness
Inverness
The Great Glen and Strathspey
A87
Aviemore
Knoydart
Cairngorms NP
Mallaig
A82
Fort William
A9
Rannoch Moor
North East Scotland
Mull
Dundee
Perth
Oban
Loch Lomond & The Trossachs NP
A9
Inveraray
Argyll and Bute
A82
Stirling
Dunoon
Central Belt
Edinburgh
Glasgow
Ayr
50 km
Campbelltown
50 mi

N

INTRODUCTION

Scotland, a land steeped in history, beauty, and legend, beckons travelers from around the world with its rugged landscapes, ancient castles, and vibrant culture. Nestled within the United Kingdom, Scotland is a country like no other, offering a unique blend of natural wonders, rich heritage, and warm hospitality.

In this captivating journey, we invite you to embark on a 10-day adventure that encapsulates a decade's worth of Scottish splendor.

"**10 Days in Scotland:** From Castles to Coastlines, A Decade's Worth of Scottish Splendor in 10 Days" is your passport to explore this enchanting nation in all its glory. Whether you are a seasoned traveler or venturing to Scotland for the first time, this book is your indispensable guide to discovering the soul of Scotland in just ten days.

As you turn the pages of this book, you'll find a meticulously crafted itinerary that takes you on a voyage through time and terrain. From the historic streets of Edinburgh to the wild and untamed landscapes of the Highlands, from the haunting ruins of ancient castles to the pristine shores of remote islands, we'll navigate the length and breadth of Scotland's diverse beauty.

But this journey is not just about ticking off tourist attractions; it's about immersing yourself in the heart of Scotland. It's about forging connections with the people, the landscapes, and the stories that have shaped this nation for centuries. It's about savoring a dram of fine Scotch whisky while listening to the haunting strains of a traditional Scottish fiddle. It's about feeling the cool mist from a cascading waterfall in the Cairngorms and exploring the eerie depths of Loch Ness.

Throughout these pages, we will introduce you to the soul-stirring experiences that await you in Scotland. You'll encounter the warmth of Scottish hospitality as you meet locals who are eager to share their tales and traditions. You'll explore the mysteries of ancient castles that have witnessed centuries of history and intrigue.

You'll revel in the breathtaking beauty of **Scotland's natural wonders,** from the tranquil shores of Loch Lomond to the dramatic cliffs of the Isle of Skye.

Each day of your journey will unveil new wonders and enrich your understanding of Scotland's past and present. Whether you have a passion for history, a love of the outdoors, an appreciation for culture, or simply a thirst for adventure, Scotland offers something for every traveler.

In this book, you'll find practical advice on everything from planning your trip and packing essentials to navigating the Scottish roadways and enjoying the local cuisine. We've included maps, tips, and recommendations to ensure your journey is as smooth as it is enchanting.

So, whether you're drawn to the ancient stones of Edinburgh Castle, the haunting beauty of Glencoe, the mystical allure of the Hebrides, or the vibrant heart of Glasgow, Scotland is waiting to capture your imagination and leave an indelible mark on your soul.

10 Days in Scotland" is your invitation to embark on a once-in-a-lifetime adventure through a land of wonder and magic. Join us as we traverse the hills and glens, follow the winding rivers, and explore the treasures that make Scotland a place like no other.

It's a journey that promises not only to fill your days with awe and inspiration but also to leave you with a deep and enduring love for this remarkable country. Welcome to Scotland, where every day is an adventure, and every moment is a memory waiting to be made.

CHAPTER 1 Day 1

ARRIVAL IN EDINBURGH

Welcome to Scotland: Immersing in a Land of Rich Heritage and Natural Beauty

As your plane touches down at Edinburgh Airport, you're about to embark on an unforgettable journey through Scotland, a land of enduring beauty and captivating history.

Your 10-day adventure begins in the heart of this enchanting country, in the capital city of Edinburgh. Today, we welcome you to the land of kilts, castles, and Celtic legends, where a rich tapestry of culture and history awaits your exploration.

Introduction to Scotland's Culture, History, and Geography

Before delving into the specifics of your Edinburgh adventure, let's take a moment to appreciate the essence of Scotland.

Nestled in the northern reaches of the British Isles, Scotland boasts a geographical diversity that ranges from rugged mountain peaks to rolling lowlands and picturesque coastlines.

This stunning terrain has not only shaped the nation's identity but also inspired countless poets, artists, and adventurers throughout history.

Scotland's culture is a vibrant tapestry woven with threads of tradition and innovation. You'll encounter proud and resilient people who have preserved their customs and heritage, from the haunting sound of bagpipes to the vibrant celebrations of the Highland Games.

The country's history is equally enthralling, with tales of ancient clans, fierce battles, and royal dynasties. The stone walls of castles and the cobbled streets of towns and cities whisper stories of centuries past.

Edinburgh: The Royal Capital

Your first day in Scotland is dedicated to exploring the magnificent city of Edinburgh, the nation's capital. Edinburgh is a city that seamlessly blends the ancient with the modern, offering a unique glimpse into Scotland's past and future.

The Historic Streets

As you step onto the cobbled streets of the Old Town, you'll feel like you've been transported back in time. The narrow alleys and historic buildings tell stories of medieval merchants, poets, and philosophers. The architecture is a blend of Gothic, Georgian, and Neoclassical styles, showcasing the city's rich architectural heritage.

The Royal Mile

Your journey begins on the Royal Mile, a bustling street that stretches from the **Palace of Holyroodhouse** at the foot of Arthur's Seat to the imposing Edinburgh Castle at its pinnacle.

Along this historic thoroughfare, you'll find an array of shops, pubs, and attractions. Don't miss the chance to visit the Real Mary King's Close, a subterranean time capsule that reveals Edinburgh's hidden history.

Iconic Landmarks

Edinburgh boasts a wealth of iconic landmarks. Your day will be incomplete without a visit to Edinburgh Castle, perched atop Castle Rock, offering panoramic views of the city.

You can explore the historic rooms, view the Crown Jewels, and witness the firing of the One O'Clock Gun.

The Palace of Holyroodhouse, the official residence of the British monarch in Scotland, is another must-visit. Stroll through its splendid State Apartments and the beautiful Holyrood Abbey ruins.

Your First Taste of Scotland

After your day of exploration, reward yourself with a traditional Scottish meal. Try haggis, neeps, and tatties—a dish that exemplifies Scottish culinary tradition—or enjoy a plate of fresh Scottish salmon or a hearty portion of fish and chips.

Accommodation options

Edinburgh offers a wide range of accommodation options to suit various preferences and budgets. Here are descriptions and locations of some popular accommodation choices in Edinburgh:

The Balmoral Hotel

The Balmoral is a luxurious and iconic hotel located at the heart of Edinburgh's city center. It boasts elegant rooms, stunning views of Edinburgh Castle, and a

Michelin-starred restaurant, Number One.

Location: 1 Princes Street, Edinburgh EH2 2EQ, United Kingdom

Website: The Balmoral Hotel

Radisson Collection Hotel, Royal Mile Edinburgh

Description: Situated on the historic Royal Mile, this modern hotel offers stylish rooms, exceptional service, and easy access to many of Edinburgh's top attractions, including Edinburgh Castle and Holyrood Palace.

Location: 1 George IV Bridge, Edinburgh EH1 1AD, United Kingdom

Website: Radisson Collection Hotel

The Witchery by the Castle

Description: This boutique hotel is famous for its opulent and romantic decor, featuring antique furnishings and rich tapestries. It's located just steps away from Edinburgh Castle and offers a unique, atmospheric experience.

Location: 352 Castlehill, The Royal Mile, Edinburgh EH1 2NF, United Kingdom

Website: The Witchery by the Castle

1.

The Scotsman Hotel

Description: Housed in a historic building, The Scotsman Hotel combines classic elegance with modern amenities. It's conveniently located near the Waverley Train Station and within walking distance of popular landmarks.

Location: 20 North Bridge, Edinburgh EH1 1TR, United Kingdom

Website: The Scotsman Hotel

Grassmarket Hotel

Description: This trendy boutique hotel is set in the lively Grassmarket area, known for its restaurants and nightlife. It offers comfortable, stylish rooms and easy access to attractions like Edinburgh Castle.

Location: 94-96 Grassmarket, Edinburgh EH1 2JR, United Kingdom

Website: Grassmarket Hotel

Apex Grassmarket Hotel

Description: Overlooking the historic Grassmarket, this modern hotel provides comfortable rooms, a rooftop terrace with stunning views, and a prime location for exploring the Old Town and Edinburgh Castle.

Location: 31-35 Grassmarket, Edinburgh EH1 2HS, United Kingdom

Website: Apex Grassmarket Hotel

These are just a few options, and Edinburgh offers a wide array of accommodations, including hotels, boutique inns, B&Bs, and apartments, to cater to various tastes and budgets. It's advisable to book your accommodation well in advance, especially during peak tourist seasons.

As you retire to your Edinburgh accommodation, let the echoes of bagpipe melodies and the memories of the day's adventures lull you into a night of anticipation for the days to come. Tomorrow, your Scottish journey continues as you delve deeper into the mysteries and wonders of this captivating country.

CHAPTER 2 Day 2

EDINBURGH'S HIDDEN GEMS

Beyond the Castle Walls: Unveiling Edinburgh's Treasures

Welcome to your second day in the historic city of Edinburgh, where you'll venture beyond the well-trodden paths and discover the city's hidden gems. Today's itinerary is all about exploring the lesser-known corners of the capital, offering you a deeper insight into the city's culture, and history, and the chance to savor Scotland's national elixir – whisky.

Discover Edinburgh's Lesser-Known Treasures

While Edinburgh Castle and the Royal Mile are undoubtedly captivating, there's much more to this city than its famous landmarks. Edinburgh is a place of secrets and surprises, and today, we're going to uncover some of its best-kept treasures.

Dean Village: Begin your day with a visit to Dean Village, a picturesque enclave hidden along the Water of Leith. Its quaint cobbled streets, charming houses, and the Dean Bridge make it a peaceful oasis in the heart of the city.

The Writer's Museum: Next, delve into Scotland's literary heritage at The Writer's Museum. This hidden gem is tucked away on Lady Stair's Close, just off the Royal Mile. Explore the lives and works of Scotland's literary giants, including Robert Burns, Sir Walter Scott, and Robert Louis Stevenson.

St. Bernard's Well: Take a stroll through the beautiful Dean Gardens and make your way to St. Bernard's Well. This neoclassical structure is nestled in the Dean Village and was inspired by the Temple of Vesta in Tivoli, Italy. It's a serene spot to enjoy a moment of reflection.

Dive into Scotland's National Drink

In the afternoon, you'll have the opportunity to experience one of Scotland's greatest contributions to the world: whisky. Edinburgh boasts a rich whisky heritage, and there's no better place to immerse yourself in this tradition than the Old Town.

The Scotch Whisky Experience: Located near the Castle, the Scotch Whisky Experience is an interactive journey through the world of Scotch whisky.

Learn about the whisky-making process, explore a vast collection of whiskies, and even take a virtual tour of Scotland's whisky-producing regions.

Whisky Tasting: After your educational tour, it's time to savor some of Scotland's finest whiskies. Choose from a selection of single malts and blended whiskies, each with its distinct flavor profile.

Whether you're a whisky aficionado or a novice, the knowledgeable staff will guide you through the tasting process.

Whisky Shops: Before you leave, consider visiting one of Edinburgh's many whisky shops to purchase a bottle of your favorite whisky as a memento of your trip.

A Night in Edinburgh's Old Town

As the day winds down, take a leisurely walk along the atmospheric streets of the Old Town, where you can admire the historic architecture, enjoy street performances, or dine at one of the city's excellent restaurants.

The enchanting ambiance of the Old
Town at night is a fitting end to your

exploration of Edinburgh's hidden gems.

Day 2 in Edinburgh has provided you with a deeper understanding of the city's cultural treasures and introduced you to the art of Scotch whisky appreciation. Tomorrow, we'll continue your Scottish adventure with a journey to the Highlands, where you'll encounter breathtaking landscapes and delve further into the country's rich history.

CHAPTER 3 Day 3

JOURNEY TO THE HIGHLANDS

Road to the Highlands: Embrace the Scenic Drive

Today marks the beginning of your voyage into the wild heart of Scotland – the Highlands.

As you depart from Edinburgh, you'll embark on a journey northward along scenic routes that showcase the country's breathtaking landscapes.

Your destination: Inverness, the gateway to the Highlands.

Start Your Journey Northward

The road to the Highlands promises not only incredible vistas but also a deeper connection to the rugged and untamed beauty that has captivated travelers for generations.

Route Options: As you depart Edinburgh, you have multiple route options to choose from. The A9, the main road north, offers a direct path to Inverness,

but consider taking detours along the way to explore hidden gems like the picturesque village of Dunkeld, home to the historic Dunkeld Cathedral.

Alternatively, take a leisurely drive through Cairngorms National Park, where you can stop to hike, view wildlife, and admire the tranquil beauty of Loch and Eilein.

Loch Ness: No journey to the Highlands is complete without a glimpse of the legendary Loch Ness.

Consider a detour to Urquhart Castle on the shores of Loch Ness for a chance to explore the ruins and, perhaps, catch a glimpse of Nessie, the elusive Loch Ness Monster.

Inverness – Gateway to the Highlands

Inverness, the capital of the Highlands, will serve as your base for Highland adventures over the next few days. This vibrant city is steeped in history and surrounded by natural wonders.

Inverness Castle: Upon your arrival in Inverness, head to Inverness Castle, an iconic red sandstone structure that overlooks the River Ness.

While the castle itself is not open to the public, its grounds offer panoramic views of the city and the surrounding countryside.

The River Ness: Stroll along the banks of the River Ness, where you'll find pleasant walking paths and charming bridges. It's a serene way to soak in the atmosphere of the city.

Exploring the City: Spend your afternoon exploring Inverness's historic streets, shops, and restaurants. The city is known for its warm hospitality and local cuisine, so be sure to savor some Highland dishes.

A Taste of Highland Culture

In the evening, consider immersing yourself in Highland culture by attending a traditional Scottish music performance at one of the local pubs or venues.

The haunting melodies of bagpipes, fiddles, and Gaelic songs will transport you deeper into the soul of Scotland.

Your first day in the Highlands has been a feast for the senses, filled with stunning landscapes and a taste of

Highland culture. Tomorrow, you'll embark on outdoor adventures in the Cairngorms National Park, where you'll have the opportunity to hike, spot wildlife, and experience the untamed beauty of the Scottish wilderness.

CHAPTER 4 Day 4

HIGHLAND ADVENTURES

Hiking the Cairngorms: Embrace the Wild Beauty of the Cairngorms National Park

Today promises to be an exhilarating exploration of the rugged and untamed landscapes of the Scottish Highlands. You'll venture into the heart of the Cairngorms National Park for an unforgettable day of outdoor adventures and, later, delve into the mysteries and folklore surrounding the legendary Loch Ness.

Embrace the Wild Beauty of the Cairngorms National Park

Cairngorms National Park: Begin your day with a drive to the Cairngorms National Park, one of the UK's most remarkable natural areas. Covering over 4,500 square kilometers of breathtaking landscapes, the

Cairngorms are a haven for nature enthusiasts and outdoor adventurers.

Hiking Trails: The park offers an array of hiking trails suitable for all levels of hikers. Whether you're a seasoned trekker or a casual stroller, you'll find a trail that suits your pace. Some popular options include:

Cairn Gorm Mountain: Ascend Cairn Gorm Mountain and experience panoramic views of the surrounding peaks and valleys.

Rothiemurchus Forest: Wander through ancient Caledonian pine forests and perhaps spot some local wildlife, including red deer and capercaillie.

Loch an Eilein: Explore the shores of Loch an Eilein, where you can take a tranquil walk around the loch and discover its picturesque island castle.

Legends of Loch Ness

In the afternoon, you'll journey southward to the renowned Loch Ness, known for its stunning beauty, and the legendary Loch Ness Monster, affectionately known as Nessie.

Urquhart Castle: Your first stop should be Urquhart Castle, strategically perched on the shores of Loch Ness.

This historic castle, once a mighty fortress, offers breathtaking views of the loch. Explore the ruins and delve into the history of this iconic site.

Loch Ness Centre & Exhibition: To learn more about the mysteries surrounding Loch Ness and Nessie, visit the Loch Ness Centre & Exhibition in the nearby village of Drumnadrochit.

Here, you'll find informative displays, films, and interactive exhibits that explore the Loch Ness Monster's legend and the science behind it.

Loch Ness Cruise: Consider taking a cruise on Loch Ness to experience the majesty of the loch up close.

While Nessie sightings are rare, the serene beauty of the loch and the surrounding mountains are more than enough to captivate your senses.

A Night on Loch Ness

In the evening, you'll have the unique opportunity to stay in accommodation along the shores of Loch Ness, where you can relax by the water's edge and perhaps catch a glimpse of the mysterious creature said to inhabit its depths. Enjoy a delicious dinner at a local restaurant while you soak in the atmosphere of this legendary place.

Day 4 of your Scottish adventure has immersed you in the wild beauty of the Cairngorms and the legends of Loch Ness. Tomorrow, your journey continues as you explore more of Scotland's dramatic landscapes and delve deeper into its rich history and culture.

CHAPTER 5 Day 5

ROAD TO THE ISLES

Glencoe: A Valley of Drama

As your journey through the Highlands continues, today's itinerary promises both dramatic landscapes and outdoor adventures. You'll explore the haunting beauty and tragic history of Glencoe before making your way to Fort William, the gateway to outdoor enthusiasts' paradise and the towering peak of Ben Nevis.

Witness the Breathtaking Beauty and Tragic History of Glencoe

Glencoe: Your day begins with a scenic drive through the breathtaking landscapes of the Scottish Highlands.

As you approach Glencoe, you'll be met with a landscape of towering peaks, deep valleys, and cascading waterfalls. This is a place where nature's drama unfolds in every direction.

Hiking in Glencoe: **To** truly immerse yourself in Glencoe's beauty, consider taking a hike in the glen.

There are several trails to choose from, catering to various skill levels. The Lost Valley hike, for instance, is a moderately challenging trek that offers spectacular views of the surrounding mountains.

The Glencoe Visitor Centre: After your hike, head to the Glencoe Visitor Centre, where you can learn about the tragic history of the Massacre of Glencoe in 1692.

Interactive displays and informative exhibits provide insight into the events that unfolded in this historic valley.

Fort William and Ben Nevis

Fort William: From Glencoe, continue your journey to Fort William, often referred to as the "Outdoor Capital of the UK." Nestled on the shores of Loch Linnhe and surrounded by stunning peaks, Fort William is a haven for outdoor enthusiasts.

Ben Nevis: Your visit to Fort William wouldn't be complete without exploring Ben Nevis, the UK's highest mountain. You can choose to hike to the summit, but this is a challenging endeavor that requires proper preparation and experience.

Alternatively, you can take the Mountain Gondola to enjoy breathtaking views of the surrounding area.

Nevis Range: If hiking Ben Nevis isn't your preference, Nevis Range offers other outdoor activities, including mountain biking, forest walks, and winter sports (seasonal). The area is perfect for those seeking adventure and breathtaking vistas without the strenuous climb.

A Night in Fort William

In the evening, you'll have the opportunity to explore Fort William further, perhaps enjoying a meal at a local restaurant or pub.

The town's picturesque location and welcoming atmosphere make it an ideal place to unwind after a day of exploration and adventure.

Day 5 of your Scottish journey has taken you through the dramatic landscapes of Glencoe and introduced you to the outdoor paradise of Fort William and Ben Nevis.

Your adventure continues tomorrow as you explore the enchanting Isle of Skye, where you'll encounter natural wonders, rich culture, and captivating beauty.

CHAPTER 6 Day 6

ISLES OF ENCHANTMENT

Crossing to Skye: Embark on a Ferry Journey to the Isle of Skye

Today marks a significant turn in your Scottish adventure as you journey to the enchanting Isle of Skye. Known for its breathtaking landscapes and rich cultural heritage, Skye is a place where nature's wonders and legends converge.

Embark on a Ferry Journey to the Isle of Skye

Ferry to Skye: Begin your day by departing from Fort William and heading to Mallaig, a picturesque fishing village on the west coast.

From Mallaig, you'll board a ferry that will transport you to the Isle of Skye. The ferry ride itself offers stunning views of the surrounding islands and the mainland.

Armadale or Kyleakin: Depending on your ferry choice, you'll either arrive in Armadale or Kyleakin. Both provide easy access to Skye's wonders. From here, you'll continue your exploration of this magical island.

Skye's Natural Wonders

The Fairy Pools: Your first stop on Skye will be the Fairy Pools, located at the foot of the Black Cuillin Mountains. These crystal-clear, blue pools and cascading waterfalls are a natural wonder. You can take a hike through the Glen Brittle forest to reach them and enjoy a refreshing dip if you're feeling brave.

The Quiraing: Next, head to the Quiraing, a unique geological formation that will leave you in awe. This otherworldly landscape features towering pinnacles, cliffs, and landslips. A hike in this area provides fantastic panoramic views.

The Old Man of Storr: Your day on Skye will culminate with a visit to the iconic Old Man of Storr.

This towering rock formation is one of Skye's most famous landmarks. A hike to the Old Man offers breathtaking views of the surrounding landscapes, including the Sound of Raasay and the Isle of Rona.

A Night on the Isle of Skye

As the day draws to a close, you'll find yourself in one of Scotland's most enchanting locations.

The Isle of Skye offers a variety of accommodations, from cozy B&Bs to luxurious hotels. Spend your evening relaxing and reflecting on the day's adventures, perhaps enjoying a traditional Scottish meal at a local restaurant.

Day 6 on the Isle of Skye has introduced you to some of the island's most captivating natural wonders. Tomorrow, your journey continues with a deeper exploration of Skye's cultural heritage, vibrant communities, and the opportunity to experience traditional music and local cuisine.

CHAPTER 7 Day 7

SKYE'S CULTURAL HERITAGE

Portree and the Isle of Skye: Discover the Colorful Harbor Town and Its Charm

Today, you'll delve into the cultural riches of the Isle of Skye, with a focus on its picturesque harbor town, Portree. You'll also have the opportunity to immerse yourself in Skye's vibrant traditions through traditional music and local cuisine.

Discover the Colorful Harbor Town of Portree

Portree: **B**egin your day with a visit to Portree, the largest town on the Isle of Skye.

This charming harbor town is known for its colorful buildings, bustling harbor, and friendly atmosphere. Stroll along the waterfront and take in the views of the bay and the surrounding hills.

Local Shops and Galleries: Portree is home to a variety of shops and galleries where you can find unique souvenirs, local artwork, and traditional Scottish crafts.

Be sure to explore the town's offerings and perhaps pick up a memento of your visit.

Experience Skye's Vibrant Culture Through Music and Food

Traditional Music: Skye has a rich musical heritage, and you'll have the opportunity to experience it firsthand. Check for local events or performances featuring traditional Scottish music, which often includes instruments like the fiddle, accordion, and bagpipes. Local pubs and cultural centers are great places to catch live music.

Local Cuisine: Skye's culinary scene is a reflection of its natural abundance. Sample local delicacies such as fresh seafood, including Skye mussels and lobster, as well as game dishes like venison. Visit a local restaurant or pub to savor these traditional flavors.

Exploring Beyond Portree

After you've had your fill of Portree's cultural offerings, consider exploring more of Skye's enchanting landscapes. The island is replete with natural wonders, from the dramatic cliffs of Kilt Rock to the scenic beauty of the Fairy Glen. These attractions offer opportunities for hikes, photography, and moments of tranquil reflection.

A Night on the Isle of Skye

As the sun sets over Skye, take the time to savor the memories of your cultural immersion and the stunning landscapes you've encountered. Whether you choose to relax in your accommodations or continue your exploration of local cuisine and music, your evening on Skye promises to be a memorable one.

Day 7 on the Isle of Skye has allowed you to connect with the island's cultural heritage and experience its vibrant traditions. Tomorrow, your journey continues as you explore more of Skye's natural wonders, including its iconic castles and pristine shores.

CHAPTER 8 Day 8

WEST COAST WONDERS

Plockton and the West Coast: Explore the Picturesque Village and Nearby Attractions

Today, your Scottish adventure takes you to the West Coast, where you'll have the opportunity to explore the charming village of Plockton and visit the iconic Eilean Donan Castle. This day promises stunning coastal scenery and a glimpse into Scotland's rich history.

Explore the Picturesque Village of Plockton

Plockton: Begin your day with a scenic drive to the village of Plockton, located on the west coast of Scotland.

Plockton is known for its stunning views of Loch Carron and its picturesque setting. As you arrive in the village, you'll be greeted by rows of charming, pastel-colored houses and a tranquil harbor.

Plockton Harbor: Spend your morning exploring Plockton's harbor area. You can take a leisurely walk along the waterfront, visit local shops and art galleries, or simply sit by the sea and soak in the peaceful atmosphere.

Plockton Palm Trees: Plockton's unique microclimate allows palm trees to thrive here, giving the village an unexpected tropical twist. These palm trees are a distinctive feature of the village and make for interesting photo opportunities.

Visit the Iconic Eilean Donan Castle

Eilean Donan Castle: After your visit to Plockton, continue your journey to one of Scotland's most iconic and photographed castles – Eilean Donan Castle. Situated on a small island in

Loch Duich, Eilean Donan is a masterpiece of medieval architecture.

Castle History: Explore the castle's rich history, which dates back to the 13th century. Learn about its strategic significance, its role in Scottish history, and its reconstruction in the 20th century. You can also visit the museum within the castle to delve deeper into its story.

Scenic Views: The castle's setting amidst the Loch Duich and surrounded by dramatic mountain scenery provides an excellent opportunity for photography.

Be sure to capture the castle's reflection in the still waters of the loch.

A Night in the Highlands

In the evening, you'll have the choice to continue your exploration of the west coast or return to your accommodation in the Highlands.

Whether you choose to dine in a local restaurant, enjoy a cozy evening by the fireplace, or stargaze under the clear Highland skies, your night in this enchanting region will be a memorable one.

Day 8 has allowed you to discover the charm of the West Coast, from the picturesque village of Plockton to the iconic Eilean Donan Castle. Tomorrow, your journey continues as you explore more of Scotland's dramatic landscapes and delve deeper into its rich history and heritage.

CHAPTER 9 Day 9

ROAD TO GLASGOW

The Scenic Drive *South: Take in the* *Beauty of Scotland's Landscapes*

Today, your Scottish journey continues as you bid farewell to the Highlands and embark on a scenic drive southward to Glasgow. Along the way, you'll have the opportunity to immerse yourself in the stunning landscapes before diving into the vibrant culture and urban energy of Scotland's largest city.

Take in the Beauty of Scotland's Landscapes

Scenic Drive: As you depart from the Highlands, you'll be treated to a breathtaking drive through Scotland's diverse landscapes. The road will lead you through rolling hills, picturesque glens, and alongside shimmering lochs. Be sure to stop at scenic viewpoints along the way to capture the beauty of the Scottish countryside.

Loch Lomond and The Trossachs National Park: Consider making a detour to Loch Lomond and The Trossachs National Park, known for its serene lochs and lush forests.

Enjoy a leisurely walk by Loch Lomond's shores or explore one of the park's hiking trails for a closer connection to nature.

Glasgow – City of Style and Culture

Glasgow: Arriving in Glasgow, you'll find yourself in a city brimming with style, culture, and history. Often overshadowed by its more famous counterpart, Edinburgh, Glasgow has a unique charm of its own.

Kelvingrove Art Gallery and Museum:
Start your exploration of Glasgow at
the Kelvingrove Art Gallery and
Museum, one of Scotland's most
popular cultural attractions. This
grand building houses a vast collection
of art and historical artifacts,
including works by renowned artists

such as Salvador Dalí and Vincent van Gogh.

Glasgow's Architecture: Glasgow is known for its striking architecture, from the Victorian and Edwardian buildings in the West End to the modern designs along the Clyde waterfront.

Take a walking tour to admire the city's diverse architectural styles, including the stunning Glasgow Cathedral and the iconic Glasgow School of Art.

Shopping and Dining: Glasgow is a shopping paradise with its stylish boutiques, bustling markets, and designer stores. Buchanan Street is a must-visit for shoppers. As evening approaches, savor a meal at one of Glasgow's trendy restaurants, where you can sample both traditional Scottish cuisine and international flavors.

A Night in Glasgow

Glasgow's vibrant nightlife offers a variety of entertainment options, from live music venues to theaters and pubs. Whether you choose to take in a show or simply enjoy a drink in a traditional Scottish pub, your night in Glasgow will be filled with excitement and cultural experiences.

Day 9 has allowed you to enjoy the natural beauty of Scotland's landscapes on your drive southward and immerse yourself in the artistic and cultural offerings of Glasgow. Tomorrow, your adventure will conclude as you reflect on your journey and make plans for future visits to this remarkable country.

CHAPTER 10 Day 10

FAREWELL TO SCOTLAND

Lasting Memories: Reflect on Your Journey and the Memories Created

As your 10-day adventure in Scotland draws to a close, take this final day to savor your experiences, create lasting memories, and plan for future journeys to this remarkable country.

Reflect on Your Journey and the Memories Created

Quiet Contemplation: Begin your day with a moment of quiet contemplation. Find a peaceful spot – perhaps a park bench overlooking a loch or a serene corner of a café – and reflect on the incredible journey you've undertaken. Think about the breathtaking landscapes, the rich history, the warm hospitality, and the people you've met along the way.

Journaling: Consider keeping a travel journal to record your thoughts, feelings, and impressions. Jot down your favorite moments, the surprises you encountered, and the lessons you've learned during your time in

Scotland. This journal will serve as a cherished memento of your journey.

Photographs: Spend some time reviewing the photographs you've taken throughout your trip. Each image tells a story, capturing the essence of Scotland's beauty, culture, and people. Relive the moments and share your favorites with family and friends.

Planning Your Return

Farewell Breakfast: Enjoy a leisurely breakfast at your accommodation, savoring the flavors of Scotland one last time. Use this time to plan your return to this enchanting country.

Future Adventures: Scotland offers a wealth of experiences and destinations that you may not have had the chance to explore during this trip. Consider creating a list of places you'd like to visit and activities you'd like to try on your next Scottish adventure.

Stay Connected: Stay connected with Scotland and its culture by joining online communities, following Scottish news, and participating in Scottish festivals or events in your home country. Learning more about

Scotland will keep your passion for this remarkable place alive until your return.

Thank You and Farewell: Take a moment to express your gratitude to the people you've met along the way – the friendly locals, fellow travelers, and those who have shared their knowledge and hospitality with you. Scotland's warm welcome is a vital part of the journey.

A Promise to Return

As you bid farewell to Scotland, remember that this is not goodbye but rather "haste ye back" – a traditional Scottish phrase that means "come back soon." Scotland's beauty, history, and culture have left an indelible mark on your heart, and your memories of this extraordinary journey will stay with you for a lifetime.

Your 10-day adventure in Scotland has been a remarkable experience filled with discovery, adventure, and cultural immersion. As you leave this land of castles, coastlines, and captivating stories, know that Scotland will always be here, waiting to welcome you back with open arms and a warm heart.

Until we meet again, farewell and safe travels!

Printed in Great Britain
by Amazon

43922833R00086